POPULAR
SONGS
HAL LEONARD
DENT PIANO LIBRARY

Piano Duets

Eight Songs for One Piano, Four Hands

Arranged by Jennifer and Mike Watts

CONTENTS

Disney and Disney/Pixar characters and artwork © Disney Enterprises, Inc.

ISBN 978-1-4803-0547-2

Walt Disney Music Company
Wonderland Music Company, Inc.

DISTRIBUTED BY

HAL•LEONARD®
CORPORATION
7777 W. BLUEMOUND RD. P.O. BOX 13819 MILWAUKEE, WI 53213

In Australia Contact:
Hal Leonard Australia Pty. Ltd.
4 Lentara Court
Cheltenham, Victoria, 3192 Australia
Email: ausadmin@halleonard.com.au

Visit Hal Leonard Online at
www.halleonard.com

The Bare Necessities

from Walt Disney's THE JUNGLE BOOK

Words and Music by
Terry Gilkyson
Arranged by Jennifer & Mike Watts

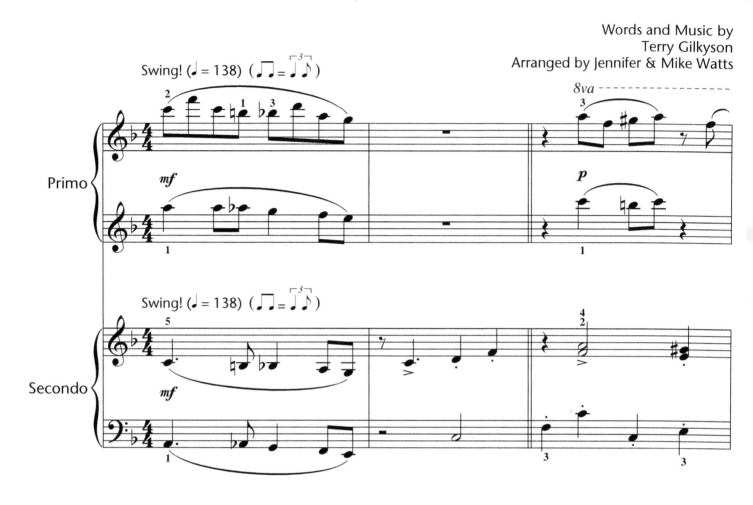

7

Belle

from Walt Disney's BEAUTY AND THE BEAST

Lyrics by Howard Ashman
Music by Alan Menken
Arranged by Jennifer & Mike Watts

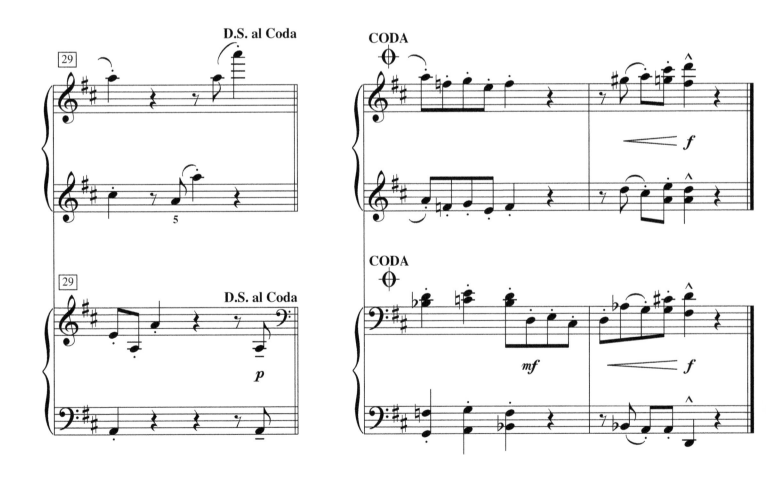

Chim Chim Cher-ee
from Walt Disney's MARY POPPINS

Words and Music by Richard M. Sherman
and Robert B. Sherman
Arranged by Jennifer & Mike Watts

16

D.S. al Coda

D.S. al Coda

CODA

CODA

Hakuna Matata
from Walt Disney Pictures' THE LION KING

Music by Elton John
Lyrics by Tim Rice
Arranged by Jennifer & Mike Watts

I See the Light

from Walt Disney Pictures' TANGLED

Music by Alan Menken
Lyrics by Glenn Slater
Arranged by Jennifer & Mike Watts

Kiss the Girl

from Walt Disney's THE LITTLE MERMAID

Music by Alan Menken
Lyrics by Howard Ashman
Arranged by Jennifer & Mike Watts

(No repeat on D.S.)

(No repeat on D.S.)

When She Loved Me

from Walt Disney Pictures' TOY STORY 2 - A Pixar Film

Music and Lyrics by
Randy Newman
Arranged by Jennifer & Mike Watts

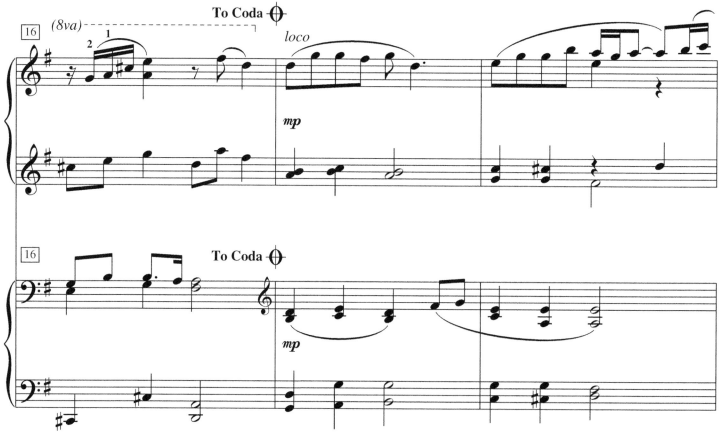

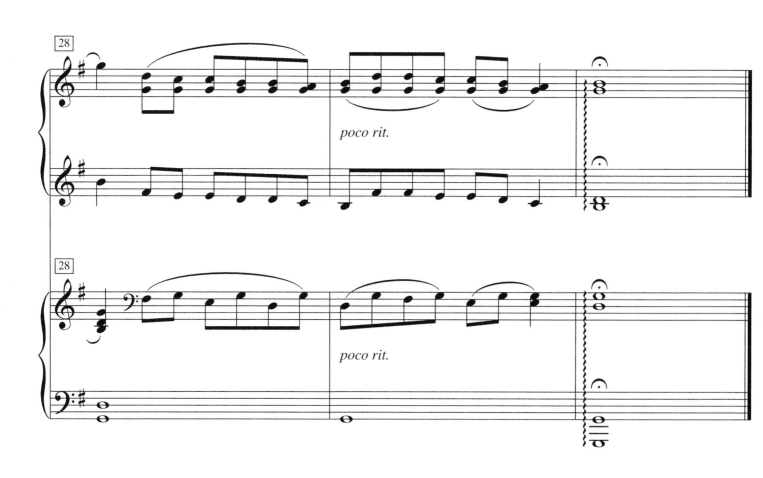

You've Got a Friend in Me

from Walt Disney's TOY STORY

Music and Lyrics by
Randy Newman
Arranged by Jennifer & Mike Watts

POPULAR SONGS
HAL LEONARD STUDENT PIANO LIBRARY

The **Hal Leonard Student Piano Library** has great songs, and yc will find all your favorites here: Disney classics, Broadway and mov favorites, and today's top hits. These graded collections are skillful and imaginatively arranged for students and pianists at every leve from elementary solos with teacher accompaniments to sophisticate piano solos for the advancing pianist.

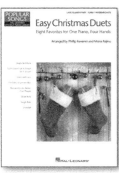

Adele
arr. Mona Rejino
Correlates with HLSPL Level 5
00159590.............................$12.99

The Beatles
arr. Eugénie Rocherolle
Correlates with HLSPL Level 5
00296649.............................$12.99

Irving Berlin Piano Duos
arr. Don Heitler and Jim Lyke
Correlates with HLSPL Level 5
00296838.............................$14.99

Broadway Favorites
arr. Phillip Keveren
Correlates with HLSPL Level 4
00279192.............................$12.99

Chart Hits
arr. Mona Rejino
Correlates with HLSPL Level 5
00296710.............................$8.99

Christmas at the Piano
arr. Lynda Lybeck-Robinson
Correlates with HLSPL Level 4
00298194.............................$12.99

Christmas Cheer
arr. Phillip Keveren
Correlates with HLSPL Level 4
00296616.............................$8.99

Classic Christmas Favorites
arr. Jennifer & Mike Watts
Correlates with HLSPL Level 5
00129582.............................$9.99

Christmas Time Is Here
arr. Eugénie Rocherolle
Correlates with HLSPL Level 5
00296614.............................$8.99

Classic Joplin Rags
arr. Fred Kern
Correlates with HLSPL Level 5
00296743.............................$9.99

Classical Pop – Lady Gaga Fugue & Other Pop Hits
arr. Giovanni Dettori
Correlates with HLSPL Level 5
00296921.............................$12.99

Contemporary Movie Hits
arr. by Carol Klose, Jennifer Linn and Wendy Stevens
Correlates with HLSPL Level 5
00296780.............................$8.99

Contemporary Pop Hits
arr. Wendy Stevens
Correlates with HLSPL Level 3
00296836.............................$8.99

Cool Pop
arr. Mona Rejino
Correlates with HLSPL Level 5
00360103.............................$12.99

Country Favorites
arr. Mona Rejino
Correlates with HLSPL Level 5
00296861.............................$9.99

Disney Favorites
arr. Phillip Keveren
Correlates with HLSPL Levels 3/4
00296647.............................$10.99

Disney Film Favorites
arr. Mona Rejino
Correlates with HLSPL Level 5
00296809 ....$10.99

Disney Piano Duets
arr. Jennifer & Mike Watts
Correlates with HLSPL Level 5
00113759.............................$13.99

Double Agent! Piano Duets
arr. Jeremy Siskind
Correlates with HLSPL Level 5
00121595.............................$12.99

Easy Christmas Duets
arr. Mona Rejino & Phillip Keveren
Correlates with HLSPL Levels 3/4
00237139.............................$9.99

Easy Disney Duets
arr. Jennifer and Mike Watts
Correlates with HLSPL Level 4
00243727.............................$12.99

Four Hands on Broadway
arr. Fred Kern
Correlates with HLSPL Level 5
00146177.............................$12.99

Frozen Piano Duets
arr. Mona Rejino
Correlates with HLSPL Levels 3/4
00144294.............................$12.99

Hip-Hop for Piano Solo
arr. Logan Evan Thomas
Correlates with HLSPL Level 5
00360950.............................$12.99

Jazz Hits for Piano Duet
arr. Jeremy Siskind
Correlates with HLSPL Level 5
00143248.............................$12.99

Elton John
arr. Carol Klose
Correlates with HLSPL Level 5
00296721.............................$10

Joplin Ragtime Duets
arr. Fred Kern
Correlates with HLSPL Level 5
00296771.............................$8

Movie Blockbusters
arr. Mona Rejino
Correlates with HLSPL Level 5
00232850.............................$10

The Nutcracker Suite
arr. Lynda Lybeck-Robinson
Correlates with HLSPL Levels 3/4
00147906.............................$8

Pop Hits for Piano Duet
arr. Jeremy Siskind
Correlates with HLSPL Level 5
00224734.............................$12

Sing to the King
arr. Phillip Keveren
Correlates with HLSPL Level 5
00296808.............................$8

Smash Hits
arr. Mona Rejino
Correlates with HLSPL Level 5
00284841.............................$10

Spooky Halloween Tune
arr. Fred Kern
Correlates with HLSPL Levels 3/4
00121550.............................$9

Today's Hits
arr. Mona Rejino
Correlates with HLSPL Level 5
00296646.............................$9

Top Hits
arr. Jennifer and Mike Watts
Correlates with HLSPL Level 5
00296894.............................$10

Top Piano Ballads
arr. Jennifer Watts
Correlates with HLSPL Level 5
00197926.............................$10

Video Game Hits
arr. Mona Rejino
Correlates with HLSPL Level 4
00300310.............................$12

You Raise Me Up
arr. Deborah Brady
Correlates with HLSPL Level 2/3
00296576.............................$7

7777 W. BLUEMOUND RD. P.O. BOX 13819 MILWAUKEE, WI 53213

Visit our website at **www.halleonard.com**